GIVE ME A
QUIET CORNER

PATIENCE STRONG

GIVE ME A
QUIET CORNER

Drawings by William Siffleet
Photographs by Ronald Goodearl and Alan Cash

Give me my scallop-shell of quiet,
  My staff of faith to walk upon,
  My scrip of joy, immortal diet,
  My bottle of salvation,
My gown of glory, hope's true gage;
And thus I'll make my pilgrimage
          Sir Walter Raleigh

FREDERICK MULLER

First published in Great Britain 1972
by Frederick Muller Ltd., 110 Fleet Street,
London, EC4A 2AP

Photographs on pages 11, 16, 18, 28 & 85 by Alan Cash; that on
page 69 by Alan Richards (courtesy Derry & Toms Ltd.); all
others by Ronald Goodearl

Printed in Great Britain by
Clarke, Doble & Brendon, Ltd.,
Plymouth

SBN 584 10755 2

CONTENTS

Give Me a Quiet Corner

GIVE me a quiet corner and a little time to hear—
the singing of the birds from dawn to dusk
throughout the year . . . Give me a chance to think
things out before it's time to go—Give me a place
where I can sit and see the sunset glow.

Give me a cottage far from all the bustle of the
town—Give me a garden I can tend until the sun
goes down . . . Give me the opportunity to see the
seasons turn—watching Nature at her work. So much
there is to learn.

Give me a window with a view that's beautiful to
see. Give me the joy of gathering my fruit from bush
and tree . . . . Give me good days and sleep-blessed
nights when I have closed the door, and anyone can
have the world. I'll never ask for more.

The Golden Leaves of Autumn

THE first green leaf that turns to gold upon the creepered wall—brings a stab of sadness for you know that it will fall—dying back into the earth from which it grew in Spring—to come back in another form when April songbirds sing.

The leaves are like the passing years of life—They come, they go. Each one has a sorrow or a blessing to bestow—and every new experience adds something to the whole—bringing wisdom, knowledge, truth, enriching mind and soul—like the fading leaf that drops to earth to fertilise—the soil in which it rests at last beneath the autumn skies.

One by one the changing years of life drop off the tree. You cannot hold one minute back whoever you may be . . . So whatever fate may do—whatever Time may bring—Face it gladly knowing God will send another Spring.

A New Road Lies Ahead

HERE where a new road you behold—Pause, remembering the old: mercies granted day by day—helping hands along the way. Providential happenings. All the good and lovely things: happy days and sunny hours—Music, friendship, gardens, flowers . . . There were clouds and sorrows too—but the good Lord gave to you—many blessings in between—blessings sometimes hardly seen.

Undeserved, you took them all. Stop a moment to recall—the pleasures that outweighed the pains—Not the losses, but the gains—looking backwards gratefully—down the track of memory . . . Drop the burden of regret. Start anew. Forgive, forget—the hurt of what was done and said—Here where a new road lies ahead.

The Dream

I LOOKED out of the window on a day of bitter cold—and on the bank between the trees I saw a flash of gold: a drift of lovely daffodils on stalks of tender green . . . But it was the winter, so a dream it must have been.

At that window once again I look out at the view —and see a sight most wonderful. My dream has all come true . . . There they are, the daffodils, beneath the apple trees—dancing to the secret music of the passing breeze.

There they are exactly as I saw them on that day —when beneath a shroud of fog the quiet garden lay . . . Spring with magic wand outstretched stands tip-toe at the door—and yet they say that miracles don't happen any more!

Flotsam

PEOPLE in a crowd like bits of flotsam seem to be
—floating on the changing tides and drifting
aimlessly . . . But who can judge? They may not be
as feckless as they seem. Maybe they are clutching at
some good and lovely dream—Or perhaps they're
lost and lonely—keeping fears at bay—Or perhaps
just happy in a simple sort of way—content to drift.
Content to move with any wind that blows. You can-
not see what lies behind a face. One never knows . . .
And those who seem the least successful may at heart
possess—the greatest blessing of this life—for what is
happiness?

Time's a Healer, So They Say

TIME'S a healer, so they say. Time can mend in Time's own way, bone and marrow torn apart, but can it mend a broken heart?

If it can, then come to me. Come and cure my malady. Come, Time, come and give relief for the gaping wound of grief. Come with days and weeks and years. Ease the pain and stay the tears. Bring the balm that soothes the mind. Time come quickly. Time, be kind. Take the sorrow from my soul. Heal my heart and make me whole.

Lamplight

LAMPLIGHT in a quiet room creates a sense of peace. The weary eyes are rested and the spirit finds release—from the agitations of the all-too-busy day. Problems merge into the shadows, trouble slips away.

In a turmoil of unrest thoughts shuttle to and fro —but if you sit with folded hands within the gentle glow—of a softly shaded lamp things happen and you find—a wonderful relaxing of the tensions of the mind.

Lamplight in a quiet room: a simple remedy—for the ills that spring from worry and anxiety . . . In a silence undisturbed there is a healing power. Many seek and find its blessing in a quiet hour.

Deep Freeze

THE earth is held a prisoner in winter's cruel vice —and in the pond the fish move blind beneath a crust of ice.

The soul is held a prisoner when friends in anger part—and love lies cold and lifeless in the unforgiving heart . . . O let the sun of kindliness shine down on all today—to soften animosity and melt old feuds away.

15

The Month I Love the Best

SEPTEMBER seemed a long way off when April blossom came—but now the creeper flushes, wine and amber, bronze and flame—and the orchard blushes where the plums and apples glow—purple, red and yellow from the branches bending low.

Ripe and rich and full of blessing are September days—the hedges bright with berries and the gardens still ablaze—with the fading splendour of the glory and the gold. The heart is well contented though the year is growing old.

This the time I love the best, the time of memory —thinking of the treasures that the months have brought to me—from the first gay crocus to the last rose withering—I count them one by one and thank the Lord for everything.

Thank You for Being a Friend

THANK you for being a friend to me when needing someone there—my failing hopes to bolster and my secret fears to share . . . Thank you for being so good to me when it was hard to know—the wisest course to follow, what to do and where to go.

Thank you for giving me confidence when I had lost my way—speaking the word that led me through the tunnel of the day . . . Thank you for all you did and said to ease the weight for me—Never intruding, but there in the background, helping quietly.

Thank you not only for sympathy in times of grief and stress—but for all you have meant to me in terms of happiness . . . Many a lovely day we've known and many a laugh we've had—Thank you for being the kind of friend that shares the good and bad.

Learning All the Time

LEARNING from each other—sifting right from wrong—trying to discover how to get along— happily together. Every day supplies—a chance for them to practise the art of compromise.

Just a married couple with their hopes and fears —making something lovely of the humdrum years . . . learning from their failures how to strike the key— that turns a note of discord into harmony.

Learning how forgiveness can make life beautiful —and how a little kindness can work a miracle— Midst their mundane problems keeping love sublime. Learning from each other . . . learning all the time.

"Be subject one to another, and be clothed with humility: for God resisteth the proud, and giveth grace to the humble."

1 Peter 5.5.

Not For Sale

NO matter what money you have in your pocket
—One moment of time you can't buy—to lock
in a cupboard and use when you need it. And oh how
the moments do fly!

You can't hoard your minutes. So whether you live
in your dotage, your teens or your prime—Pray that
the good Lord will give you the wisdom of knowing
the value of time.

Lord I Cannot Understand

LORD, I cannot understand. It's all too much for
me. Underneath the music there's a note of
tragedy—But it comforts me to know that all things
everywhere—rest within the circle of Thy provi-
dential care.

Life and death are part of an eternal mystery. The
future is uncertain and the end I cannot see—but all
I need to know is this: that there's a God above—
who leads the faithful through the darkness and His
name is Love.

The Surprise

A STREAK of gold lies bright as flame across the melting snow—where a drift of crocuses with chalices aglow—open wide their shining cups to catch the morning light—I look at them amazed although it's such a common sight.

All along suburban streets the passer by can see— little crocus patches, mauve and chrome and ivory . . . In city park and country garden everywhere they rise —year by year and yet they always take me by surprise.

Every coming is a kind of miracle to me—something in the nature of a holy mystery . . . That is why when first they come to shine around my door—I stare as if I'd never seen a crocus there before.

Love Makes All Things Possible

BEAR with them who bear a cross and sympathetic try to be. Gently deal with the afflicted, for you cannot know or see—what the hidden trouble is beyond the reach of human skill . . . Though demanding tact and patience and an effort of the will—keep a hold upon yourself and pray for grace to carry through—kindly and with understanding everything you have to do.

People may be difficult—but every person is unique: sick or healthy, young or aged, smart or simple, strong or weak—Precious in the sight of God —So if He places in your care—one of His unhappy creatures, do not fail Him. Try to bear—the brunt of it with cheerfulness. Though sorely tried, be merciful. Love will lighten every task, for Love makes all things possible.

He Knows it All

HE knows how long a road can be for He with strength far spent—walked the road to Calvary with blood-stained shoulders bent—beneath the cross from which He was to hang by nail-pierced hands. He knows how long a road can be . . . He knows and understands.

He knows how words can wound the soul and how a heart can bleed—for He Himself has known the pang of every human need . . . He knows the sort of loneliness that none on earth can share. He knows the weight of every cross and how much we can bear.

He knows the measure of a man and what within him lies. He knows how deeply we can sink and how far we can rise . . . He knows it all: the strain, the heartbreak and the weariness. That is why He has the power to save and heal and bless.

The Flame

HAPPINESS is like a candle flame—that flickers in a draught and loses light . . . A breath of disapproval or of blame—dims the lovely glow, however slight.

Check the word that dissipates the joy. Shield the gentle flame that warms the heart—lest a little passing breeze destroy—the precious peace . . . and Love itself depart.

Let the candle of your happiness—keep its brightness, burning steadily . . . Let it shine in times of storm and stress—undisturbed amidst adversity.

England's Garden

WHEN you think of orchards then your thoughts go wandering—to the place where seas of blossom lap the lanes of Spring . . . England's garden. Once a little kingdom by the sea—where the white cliffs guardian stand as if to keep us free.

Hops and cherries, sheep and apples, corn and cricket field. Canterbury, Dover, Hythe, the Medway and the Weald. Churches old as Christendom. Preserve from the intent—of planners who would spoil the good and lovely land of Kent.

A Touch of
Magic

THERE'S a touch of magic in this little miracle. A fairy must have waved a wand for something wonderful—has happened by the cottage gate—a small flower bridal-white—has come up through the frosted earth and almost overnight—spread around the apple tree. It happens every year—but it is always a surprise when suddenly they're here!

Close to earth they hang their heads as if they were afraid—to anticipate too much. The wind is like a blade—cutting through the leafless hedge and so they hesitate—peeping round uncertainly like strangers at a gate.

Come on little snowdrops there's a greeting here for you—though up in that wintry sky there's not a fleck of blue . . . You are more than welcome on this bleak and bitter day—for when once you come we know that Spring is on the way.

The Seasons of
the Heart

JUST as the year has its cycle of seasons, the heart
has its seasons and changes of mood. Moments of
doubt when we walk in the shadows. Moments of
glory when hope is renewed.

Just as the earth on its diurnal journey turns its
bright face to the dark of the night, the heart plunges
down into grief and regretting, away from the source
of its life and its light.

Nothing is permanent. All things are passing.
Hopelessness, happiness, pleasure and pain. Stand still
and wait for the change of the season. God never fails
to send springtime again.

The Good Years Come

THE good years come, the good years go—filled with quiet content. We scarcely heed them as they pass: the years from Heaven sent—full of blessings, seldom noticed, taken thanklessly. It's only when the good years end that we can truly see—the joy of things that left no trace—when life moved at an even pace.

The bad years come, the bad years go, but these leave marks behind—scars of bitter memory engraved upon the mind: the years that stab the heart awake —when trouble comes to you, as come it must to everyone—but somehow we get through . . . The bad years go, but when the good return give God the praise. Remember and be grateful for the uneventful days.

Learning How
to Live

DON'T expect too much, too soon, of all that life can give. First you must be taught your lessons, learning how to live—not for trivial things alone, small aims and selfish ends, but doing what you can to help your neighbours and your friends.

So if plans are thwarted and you feel misunderstood—do not be surprised or hurt, but take the bad and good—in your stride, not always reaching out for happiness, but thankful for whatever comes to comfort, heal and bless . . . If you try to cultivate a grateful frame of mind—many mercies you will have and many blessings find.

Never Give Up

FOLLOW what the inner voice is saying. Never give up hope but keep on praying . . . Wonders did not cease in Galilee. Jesus said, The Truth shall make you free.

When you're faced with that which spells disaster —Nothing fear. Remember mind is master . . . Though success may seem impossible—Every day expect a miracle.

Sky

PITY those for whom there is no sky. No stars, no sun, no white clouds drifting by—but just a dead white ceiling overhead—to look at from the prison of a bed.

When you walk, look up and thankful be—even though no glint of gold you see . . . You are blessed if on the earth you tread—with nothing but the sky above your head.

The Rose that Lingered On

THE rose that lingered on into November—a lovely bloom of crimson and of gold—warmed my spirit like a glowing ember—amongst a heap of ashes grey and cold.

The rose that lived to see the green leaves turning —was like a breath of June that brought to me— recollections of a bright sun burning—on lily, iris, phlox and peony.

The rose that lingered on into November—conjured from the blue autumnal haze—the summer that I always shall remember: the summer of the happy, happy days.

Needing Each Other

THE child looks at the full-grown man—and says, Please tell me if you can—the way if Truth I am to find. I need the wisdom of your mind—and all the guidance you can give—if happily I am to live.

The man looks in the child's bright eye—and says, Please tell me how can I—regain the simple faith I knew—when I was young and small, like you, recapturing the radiance—of the years of innocence?

Both have much to teach and learn—from one another. Each can turn—to the other, finding Truth. Youth needs age and age needs Youth.

Above Funchal

BLAZE of petals, fiery red against a sky of corn-
flower blue . . . In a street of shuttered windows
blaze of beauty blinding you.

Glimpse of garden through the pattern of a grille
of iron wrought—fan of blossom on a terrace in a web
of shadows caught.

Here where London grey and wintry chills the flesh
and bites the bone, I am warmed, remembering the
glow of flowers on sun-baked stone.

Trees

WHAT would life be like without the trees—with
no green leaf to quiver in the breeze—To cast
a cooling shadow on the grass—and mark the chang-
ing seasons as they pass?

Imagine towns with no old tree to spread—a
canopy of branches overhead: a tree with boughs out-
stretched towards the sky—as if to bless the people
rushing by.

The Immortal Few

PROUD are we who can remember that historic
hour—when Youth against the might and fury
of Germanic power—flew into the fires of hell all
Christendom to save—Proud are we, remembering
the young, the gay, the brave.

Battle of the British Islands fought out in the sky!
The fight that wrought a miracle. O let it never die:
the memory of those who bought us time to rise anew.
Honoured be their names forever: the immortal few.

On the Rocks

WHEN your ship is caught in stormy weather—
Your marriage on the rocks about to sink—
Why not try a little prayer together—Praying slows
you down and makes you think.

Never sail full steam towards disaster—saying
something that will leave a scar—If you let your anger
be the master—You will lose control and go too far.

Pause before the best of life is broken—Remember
how you loved and how you smiled . . . Save the
wreck. Let words of peace be spoken—that bring
you back to harbour, reconciled.

Hope and Faith Together

E VEN though your hopes no sign of fruit or flower-
ing show. Tend them with a daily prayer and
God will make them grow. Hope and faith together
working make a miracle. To the heart that never
doubts all things are possible.

Though your faith be like a lamp that flickers in
the night, hope will feed the dying flame and keep
the wick alight. Hope and faith when linked together
working hand in hand, work the wonders of the Lord
because they can command mighty forces stronger
than the puny powers of man, working through the
laws of God according to His plan. Healing, saving,
re-creating; making all things new. Proving by results
that every Word of God is true.

The Song the Silence Sings

SILENCE is the language of the heart—when sorrow comes and dearest souls depart—For who can speak the word that can express—the agonies of loss and loneliness?

So listen to the song the silence sings—and rest upon the comfort that it brings . . . It's only when the human voices cease—that you can hear the Voice that giveth peace.

There's More to Life than Getting On

THERE'S more to life than getting on, making money, having fun. There's more to life than what you see—this side of eternity.

There's more to life than meets the eye—so do not let the years slip by—and never pause to look below the surface of the passing show.

A man-made world is very small. You never really live at all—until you've found a God to shed—a glory round the path you tread.

Never Before

NEVER before have you ever seen this date upon the calendar. Never before have you ever passed this way . . . Never before have you trodden here. New is this moment of the year. Never before have you ever lived to-day.

Never before. It's a gift that is as fresh as morning dew. How will you use what it brings of boon or bane? . . . O what a day this day might be: a glorious opportunity—to cut your losses and begin again!

Somebody said that somebody said

SOMEBODY said that somebody said. Trouble was caused and suspicion fed. Somebody passed on an idle word. Someone repeated what someone had heard.

There has been many a broken heart. Many a marriage has come apart. Many relationships have been changed. Many a neighbour become estranged. In many a home where peace once reigned affection and loyalty have been strained, and many a life is incomplete all because someone was indiscreet.

Many a friendship has been wrecked—through gossip unfounded and unchecked. Mischief was made and a rumour spread. Somebody said that somebody said.

To Remember

DO not let the greyness of November—seep into the corners of your mind—There is always something to remember—something that the summer leaves behind.

The garden: lilac, lavender and roses. Holidays: the country and the sea—recollect anew as autumn closes—and live again your lovely memory . . . Grim and grey the outlook in November—but there's always something to remember.

A Bunch of Rosebuds

SOMEONE brought her rosebuds when she was lying ill, and, as she watched them in the bowl upon the window-sill, she thought of all the blessings that their sweetness had bestowed. First on the grower, then on those who saw them from the road—glancing in the florist's window as they hurried by. The touch of beauty to the soul and pleasure to the eye.

What a joy it must have been to buy them and to bring such loveliness to someone laid aside by suffering. Everyone who looked at them was blessed in some strange way and, when the petals fell and they had had their little day, their mission was fulfilled . . . Into a world of storm and stress they had breathed the breath of peace and brought much happiness.

Think Happiness

THINK health, think hope, think happiness—and in a wondrous way—things will work out for your good. Though dreary be the day—you will see a shaft of sunlight breaking through the cloud—as you walk with shoulders squared, heart light and head unbowed.

Others bound by grievances are bent with worldly care—but you'll be free and you will see a glory everywhere—raising hands to catch the many blessings as they fall: the manna God still sends to be enjoyed and shared by all.

The Greatest Gift

GIVE your children little things and not expensive toys. Teach them to appreciate small gifts and simple joys . . . Try to make them understand that money does not drop—out of heaven, nor can it be purchased at a shop.

Money must be earned and never wasted. Let them know—that Love inspires the giving of the presents we bestow—and the greatest gift that you could ever give to them—is a faith that leads them to the Babe of Bethlehem.

Luck

LUCK is never in or out because there's no such thing. Thoughts and actions, right and wrong, their own rewards will bring . . . Consequences good and bad from what you do you draw. What you call your luck is just the working of a law.

Sometime, somewhere, somehow you will reap with joy or tears—the rich or meagre harvests of the unforgiving years . . . Don't believe in luck. Believe in God. Employ your will—to do what's right. The power is yours to use for good or ill.

A Tree is a Good Companion

A TREE is a good companion as seasons come and go—In spring the trees burst into leaf and set the heart aglow—with resurrected life and when the summer comes again—they spread a kindly tent of shade in park and country lane.

In autumn they are lovely: flame, copper, gold and red. Silently upon the earth their dying leaves they shed—giving us the peace we need to walk life's crowded maze—facing with tranquillity the threat of harder days.

And when the branch is bare they stand resigned to winter's thrust—teaching us to hoard our strength and wait with quiet trust . . . A tree is a good companion if days be dark or fair. Impersonal, and yet your every mood it seems to share—always there to meet your need, to comfort and to bless—a secret source of consolation and of happiness.

Look at Roses

IF your faith has faltered and God seems unreal to you—Look at roses and you'll know that everything is true . . . In park or garden take a walk and you will surely find—a lovely and a living proof of the creative Mind—of Him who made the sun, the moon, the water and the land. Look at roses freshly come from the Creator's hand . . . White and crimson, gold and lemon, apricot and flame. Every fragrant bud and bloom outbreathes His Holy name.

Look at roses when oppressed by weariness or grief. Look at roses and restore spent hope and lost belief— in the meaning of this life and of a Heaven above. Look at roses if you ever doubt that God is Love.

The Last Straw

IT'S the little things that stab the heart—that dim the light of life and turn it grey . . . It's the thoughtless act that tears apart—the finely woven fabric of the day.

It's the tiny straw that breaks the back—when added to the daily wear and tear . . . It's the extra feather in the sack—that makes the burden more than you can bear.

So check yourself before you say too much. You may be right, but exercise control . . . Another word could be the final touch: the straw that breaks the overburdened soul.

Before the Storms Begin

WHEN a storm assaults a tree it's the weakest boughs that fail. It's the rotten branch that crashes in the fury of a gale.

When the storms of life come raging—bringing ruin in their train—It's the point where faith is weakest that collapses with the strain . . . Daily look to your defences—and where time has worn them thin —mark the place that needs repairing—and before the storms begin—do the work of restoration. Do it now. A good job make—for when searching winds come blowing it's the weakest boughs that break.

Under Snow

UNDER rain, they say, there's famine—poverty and dearth—ruin lies beneath the heavy weight of rain-soaked earth—but under snow, they say, there's bread. The bulb, the seed, the root. The harvest of the coming summer, corn and flowers and fruit.

Snow when crusted thick with ice looks cold and merciless—but in truth the falling flakes are sent to warm and bless—spreading a protective carpet on the open land—preserving life within the soil from winter's cruel hand.

Underneath the snow within an iron-hard moulding set—lies the fragile beauty of the woodland violet: the golden-throated daffodils that in the March winds blow—sleep beneath the gentle pressure of the kindly snow.

One Fine Day

ONE fine day you'll wake and find that everything's all right—you will wonder why you worried, struggling day and night—to unravel knotted cords and tangled threads of fate—doing what you thought was best and putting matters straight.

Wondering how things could ever work out right for you—with nobody to share the load and not a hope in view—of happier tomorrows. Just you wait and you will see—Better days are on the way. The best is yet to be.

How's it going to happen? Never mind. That's God's affair. He is in control. Whatever comes. He'll get you there. Never say you're beaten. Lift your head and go your way. Faith will bring its own reward. Just wait and trust and pray.

Echoes in a Quiet Room

I SIT in a web of shadows—and the clock in sleepy mood—wakens the sense of magic that comes with solitude . . . I hear—or I dream I'm hearing beyond its fairy chimes—the echo of lost enchantments and music of gracious times.

The whisper of silks and satins. The tones of an old spinet. The footsteps of stately figures, dancing a minuet . . . The tinkle of crystal glasses. The laughter, like silver bells. The voices as soft and lovely as murmur of waves in shells.

The swish of a fan unfolding. The clink of a jewelled chain. You ask is it fact or fancy. The mystery must remain . . . I and the clock know the answer, but the secret we must keep. We know what we hear in the stillness when the old house falls asleep.

On Trial

WE'RE on trial and everything that happens day by day—puts us to the test in what we do and what we say . . . Circumstances weigh us in the balance of events—in small affairs that seem to be of little consequence—and important matters when we're hurt or driven hard. We are judged by what we are when we are off our guard.

Never does the devil give up fighting for a soul—or lose a chance to undermine and break down self-control. Fools deny that he exists, but every passing hour—proves how much we need to guard against the evil power—that lies in wait to trick us, to deceive and to destroy—our faith, our hope, our peace of mind, our courage and our joy . . . There is no escaping. Every day is judgment day—That is why the Master said that we should watch and pray.

The Power Within

THERE is something in your mind beyond the conscious brain—that can solve your problem if quiescent you remain . . . If you struggle—round and round your troubled thoughts will spin—never getting anywhere . . . so trust the power within—to find the right solution and to work the whole thing out. Stop worrying, stop wondering. Get off the roundabout.

Shelve your problem for the moment. Try and let it be. Tomorrow or the next day you will wake and you will see—the answer to the question and the road ahead will run—straight and clear and prove to be the best for everyone . . . Worry is destructive—but your battle you will win—if you pray for guidance and you trust the power within.

If You Knew How Many Years

IF you knew how many years of living lay ahead—
you'd treasure every pleasure—if you knew . . .
If you knew the measure of the road you had to tread
—the world would seem a sweeter place to you.

The grass would be a brighter green, the rose would
lovelier grow—the birds a more ecstatic song would
sing—if you knew how many times you'd watch the
summer go—and see the winter vanish into spring.

If you knew how many times you'd see the fairy
lace—of spider webs on dewy grass unfold . . . You
would see a greater beauty in the commonplace—
and hoard the days as misers hoard their gold.

There's Always a Way

THERE'S always a way to put things right when everything seems wrong—if the good intent is there and if the will is strong—strong enough to thrust away the thoughts that stab and sting—to forgive and to forget the hard and hurtful thing.

There's always a way to move the mountains and of getting through—obstacles and difficulties looming up at you . . . There's always a way of changing discord into harmony—and smoothing off the sharpest edge of animosity.

All too often do we let the evil forces win—just because we fail to let the power of love flow in . . . Love is reconciliation, but it cannot be—unless we learn the simple lesson of humility . . . Pride erects its barriers, but Love comes breaking through—the enclosures of resentment, making all things new.

Black Lace

WHEN through trees the sifted sunlight falls—it makes a lovely pattern on the walls—of leaf-shaped shadows black as ebony—on a screen of gold and ivory.

Later comes the moonlight through the tree—and again that pattern I can see—as if an artist's hand had draped a shawl—of black and silver lace across the wall.

All Day Long

ALL day long a blackbird sang. All day long the garden rang—with notes that fell like silver spray—on the lilac and the may . . . Was it just a common bird—made the music that I heard—or did angels hovering, teach the blackbird how to sing—and human beings how to to say—Thank you for a lovely day?

A Garden in the Sky

HIGH above the busy road in crowded Kensington—there's a garden in the sky. The sun looks down upon—roses, pansies, irises and scented alyssums—lavender, lobelia and gay geraniums. Fuchsias set in stately urns down pathways green and cool. Willows, palms and pink flamingoes by a shady pool . . . Spring comes here as surely as it comes to country ways—with apple blossom, daffodils and tulips all ablaze.

Strange to think a great store stands beneath these leafy bowers. People buy and sell below the roots of trees and flowers. Up above the traffic there is music to be heard: the tinkling of a fountain and the fluting of a bird . . . Art and Nature have conspired this lovely place to make. Beauty waits to meet the eye with every step you take: the lily floating on the pond, the silver waterfall. The well, the bell, the terrace; and the vine upon the wall.

Troubles are forgotten as you wander up and down —the quiet paths that wind above the roar of London town . . . This was one man's happy thought fulfilled as time went by. One man's vision. One man's dream: a garden in the sky.

To the Young

IF there seems to be no meaning in the life you lead
—If you have no dreams to dream, no purpose
and no creed—it's because within your mind there is
a vacancy—a vacuum, an emptiness, a space where
God should be.

Youth needs something greater than a man-made
world can give—something greater than itself for
which to work and live: the hardship of a task that
calls for faith and energy—the challenge of a gospel
that demands self-mastery.

Through the cheap and easy freedoms of this law-
less age—we have robbed the youngsters of their
Christian heritage . . . We have soured the wine of
life and failed them utterly—by crucifying once
again the Christ of history.

Testing Times

HOLD on in the darkness though no gleam of light breaks through. Keep on dreaming dreams although they never quite come true . . . Keep on moving forward though you don't know what's ahead. Keep on keeping on though it's a lonely road you tread.

Keep on looking up towards the goal you have in view. Keep on at the task that God has given you to do. Keep on in the hope that there are better times in store. Keep on praying for the thing that you are waiting for.

Blessings come to those who in the turmoil of events —seek to see the goodness of the will of Providence . . . Hold to this and never doubt. Keep head and spirits high. You'll discover that the storm was only passing by.

See Life as a Whole

DON'T expect the sun to shine each hour of every day—then you won't be disappointed when the skies go grey . . . If we never had the rain we'd never have the bloom—so when weather's bad don't let it plunge you into gloom.

This applies to life as well. You can't expect the years to run on smoothly bringing you all laughter and no tears . . . Joys and sorrows balance if they're rightly understood— so when things go wrong don't lose your faith in what is good.

Know your cares are passing by like clouds above your head. Believe that all is well, and through your troubles you'll be led . . . See life as a whole. Pray not for freedom from distress—but for grace to weigh the hurts against the happiness.

The Memory

LIFE takes much away from us as through the years we go—changes come with changing times. We know it must be so . . . But no matter what may come you keep the precious key—to the private treasure-house we call The Memory.

Nothing that the world can do can rob you of the joy—of recollections life could never fade nor Time destroy. They are yours forever. In your mind you have the power—to resurrect the lovely moment and the golden hour.

What it is or how it works could never be explained —in spite of all the progress made and all the knowledge gained . . . Through the door of memory the past you can renew: a secret world that nobody can take away from you.

Regrets

THE moment you missed when the chance came along—to mend an old quarrel or right an old wrong—The times that you doubted when troubles. you met . . . These are the things you regret.

The word of forgiveness you failed to express. The waste of life's goodness—the lost happiness. The hurt that you could not or would not forget . . . These are the things you regret.

Magic Carpet

INTO the projector slip the small transparency—
and like a journey on a magic carpet you can be
—carried back in memory to summer holidays . . .
Not in realms of fantasy, but there before your gaze
—you can see in all the colours of reality—the
country lanes, the city streets, the mountains and the
sea.

The blue of an Italian sky, the red of Devon sand
—the paradise of Scotland's isles and Wordworth's
wonderland. The stately homes of England and the
grey old market towns: the abbeys, the cathedrals,
Kentish orchards, Sussex downs.

Wales: the mountain pasture and the silver water-
fall. Is it not a miracle to flash upon a wall—a pic-
ture bringing summer back when outside in the rain
—the winds of winter howl like wolves around the
windowpane.

The Mercy Stroke

WHEN fate inflicts a bitter blow that robs life of its zest it's hard to think how it could ever turn out for the best. Blind with tears, you cannot see the pattern of events time is weaving on the secret looms of Providence.

But when the years have done their work and when the wound has healed, to the eye of faith the hidden purpose is revealed. The unexpected thing that struck as if by cruel chance, proves to be the guardian angel of deliverance. When you live no longer under Sorrow's heavy yoke, you will see the loving hand behind the mercy stroke.

Faith

ALL is dark for you today. No ray of hope you see. But wait a little longer. Wait and trust and there will be—an answer to the problem and an easing of the pain. You will turn a corner and begin to live again.

Thought has power, so think yourself into a hopeful mood. Though today you see no cause for joy or gratitude . . . Faith moves mountains. For with God all things are possible. Every morning lift your heart. Expect a miracle.

Serenity

DO not force the pace of life, though much you have to do. Take some time for being quiet. a minute, maybe two—to make a break from all that drives you on from day to day. Give yourself a chance to stop, to think, perhaps to pray.

You need to soothe the jangled nerves and calm the worried mind. To ease the overburdened heart, to rest and to unwind . . . Find a peace within yourself and stronger you will be—having learned the precious secret of serenity.

If Trouble Never Came Your Way

IF life were all felicity—there would be no Calvary. If this our world were Paradise—there'd be no call for sacrifice. No spur of faith to drive you on—when the last faint hope had gone . . . If no one ever had to bear—a heavy cross—How could you share —another's grief, for there would be little need for sympathy.

Wisdom comes through suffering. Tragedies much grief may bring—but a heart is like a stone if a heart has never known—the desperation of despair—the consolation of a prayer—for these things if understood—can be used and turned to good. Thus we grow. Without the pain—static would the mind remain.

If life were perfect how should we—find the opportunity—to help a neighbour on the road—to lend a hand and ease a load. If trouble never came your way—you'd never feel the need to pray.

The Harvesting

DO not lose faith when you are down—and place the blame on God for everything . . . Our tragedies and trials are mainly due—to ignorance and human blundering.

We disregard the Biblical design—for happiness, for health and harmony . . . We break His laws then wonder why we reap—a bitter harvest of adversity

Have a Lovely Holiday

HAVE a lovely holiday. Enjoy it and come back —eager to set out once more along the daily track—having had your strength recharged to start your life anew—feeling fine and ready for the job you have to do.

Have a lovely holiday. Relax and let your mind—bask in peace with all the woes and worries left behind. Do not go for pleasures that belong to the routine—seated at the wheel or by a television screen.

Give yourself a change and get away from crowds and fumes—go on foot where silence reigns and where the wild flower blooms—Fill your lungs with air as God intended air should be: pure and healthy, blowing from the hills or from the sea . . . Come back happy, come back well, in mind and body fit. Have a lovely holiday and make the most of it.

Believe

LIFE could be so simple, so happy and so good—if only we would live the Master's creed . . . Be like little children. If that were understood—a loving God would meet our every need.

We create our problems, our trouble and our pain because this simple truth we can't receive—Worldly wisdom fails us, but true His words remain . . . Be like little children—and believe!

Time in Hand

WHEN a busy day you've planned—give yourself some time in hand—so that jobs don't overlap. Try to leave a little gap between the things you have to do—a tiny pause enables you—to get your balance with no need—to rush around at breakneck speed—never poised or punctual. Try to make an in-interval—so that there is time to spare—instead of hurrying everywhere.

Sometimes it's beyond your power—to arrange a crowded hour—in a way that leaves a break—giving you a chance to take—a few brief moments to unwind. To be ahead and not behind—thus conserving energy—for the next activity . . . Up to most things you can stand—if you have some time in hand.

Before you Blame Another

BEFORE you blame another take a look inside your mind. Search your thoughts and if you're honest maybe you will find—you too made mistakes and were not always wholly wise. Try to see the picture through the other person's eyes.

Whether you were in the wrong or whether in the right—Second thoughts will sometimes throw a new and different light—on a situation that has hurt and troubled you. Try to change your attitude and shift your point of view.

Get it from another angle and perhaps you'll see —where you brought the discord in that spoilt the harmony . . . Were you too to blame for all the heartache and distress? Ask yourself before you wreck your future happiness.

Investments

LIFE is like a bank in which your good deeds you
invest. They will swell your capital and truly
you'll be blessed—and enriched from day to day with
handsome dividends—in the form of happiness, con-
tentment, and good friends.

Cynicism, selfishness and sins of every kind—rob
you of your substance and impoverish the mind . . .
If you would enjoy the fruits of joy and peace and
health—keep on adding to your secret hoard of in-
ward wealth.

Sacrifices made for others golden profits show.
Every selfless action on the credit side will go—God
supplies the needs of those who meet another's lack.
Draw from life—but what you take, remember to put
back.

Two Blind Eyes

LIKE the owl, it's sometimes wise—to look at things with two blind eyes. Though it may be plain as day—you often find that it will pay—Not to see and not to hear—what to others may be clear. If you cannot help or mend—it is wiser to pretend—You're not always in the right, Nor can you always trust your sight.

This is wisdom. Learn to know—when to come and when to go. When to say what's on your mind—and when to be both deaf and blind—trying not to criticize, but to turn unseeing eyes—on what other people do—when it hurts or angers you . . . Where there's animosity—it's sometimes better not to see— then there's nothing to regret—to forgive or to forget.

Experiment

TODAY make this experiment and do what you were told—To love your neighbour as yourself instead of being cold—indifferent or critical. Try out the Master's way. Make the great experiment and do it now—today.

This they say will make you happy. Find out if it's true. It has worked for other people. Make it work for you—Instead of going through the day at odds with everyone. Apply the golden rule of love and prove it can be done.

Watch the frowns turn into smiles. You'll be surprised to find—how a friendly answer blunts the edge of words unkind . . . Life is big, so why be small? A good world it could be. Try today the Christian way of grace and charity. Jesus came to show us how to live and how to die. It's the only way that makes life work—so why not try?

Pause

PAUSE when you are undecided on the course to take. Pause when you are flustered and a quiet moment make. Pause to calm the troubled mind and ease the sense of strain. Pause to rest the jangled nerves, your balance to regain.

Pause before you do the thing that leaves an ugly scar. Pause before you lose your grip and anger goes too far . . . Pause before you say the word that breaks a human tie. Pause a little, long enough to let the storm blow by.

Remember What Went Right

WEIGH the good against the bad, the worst against the best. You've been hurt, but you've been helped and have you not been blessed? . . . There were times when skies were dark, but often they were bright. There were storms, but in the end a rainbow came in sight.

You have had your troubles but you've had the good days too. Much you lost, but many mercies have been granted you . . . Problems there are bound to be. Life can't be all delight. When you think of what went wrong remember what went right.

Dream Garden

THE lawn is just like velvet across the garden spread—smooth and green and lovely—no daisy rears its head . . . In the well-kept borders the flowers like rainbows glow—No deaths, no disappointments, no weed to mar the show.

The roses are exquisite and better than the best—improving on perfection—No threat of blight or pest . . . The orchard blooms unfailing and in their seasons come—cherry, apple, greengage, damson, pear and plum.

There's no need to tell you it's only in the mind. Just imagination. You'd never ever find—a work-free weed-free garden. Impossible it seems—but in spite of everything we go on dreaming dreams—of the flawless blossom and the perfect rose—from the spring's beginning to the autumn's close.

Today

DO not bank upon tomorrow. Do your best today. Maybe there's a future, maybe not, for who can say? The present is the only time you can be sure about—if you have a demon now's the time to cast it out.

Now's the moment for improvement. Now's the time to make—something better of yourself and now's the time to take—stock of what you're like behind the face you show your friends. Now's the golden moment. Now's the time to make amends.

October

WE do not leap from summer into winter's cruel grip—scarcely noticing the changes, day by day we slip—into autumn's gentle mood and quietly we are led—through the lanes where turning leaves glow russet, gold and red.

Kindly is the English climate. Lovely are the links —between the changing seasons . . . As the year in passing sinks—into the engulfing fogs, cold winds and frosty glaze—we walk enchanted through the magic of October days.

Never a Moment

TOO many roads to explore. Too many battles to fight. Too many rings at the door. Too many things to put right . . . Too many problems to face—too many irons to heat. Too many pleasures to chase. Too many people to meet.

Too many phone calls to make. Too many errands to run. Too many journeys to take. Too many jobs to be done . . . Too many worries that grind—round in your brain like a mill. Too many things on your mind. That's why you never sit still.

Too many mountains to climb. Too many dates to fit in—That's why you never find time—to look for the treasures within—cramming too much in a day—with never a moment to pray.

Every Year At Winter's Ending

YEAR by year I've seen the catkins on the hazel bough. Year by year I've watched the seagulls following the plough. Year by year I've marked the yellow crocus thrusting through. Yes, I've seen it all before, but every time it's new.

Every time the heart beat quickens at the lovely sight—of the flowering almond trees and lilacs mauve and white . . . Every time it happens it's as if God said to me—Behold! I make a miracle for everyone to see.

Every year at winter's ending when the blackbird sings—and the rosy budded hedges are alive with wings—the old sweet wonderment comes back, half rapture and half pain—and, like the earth with life renewed, I too am young again.